PLAY CHAMPIONSHIP GOLF

He can pin a man to the floor without touching him. He can stand on one foot and hold off twenty-two power lifters and professional football players. Now, Richard Behrens, one of the foremost martial arts masters in the world, brings the game of golf to exciting new dimensions with his revolutionary physical and mental techniques for strength, power, and accuracy.

You will learn how to improve your game beyond your wildest dreams; from mind basics, to developing true power, to achieving "the zone." Enjoy greater accuracy both off the tee and from the fairway, hit more green in regulation, and lower your average number of putts per round.

Try just one principle at a time. You'll find that your game improves on the first day out! By the time you have incorporated all of the techniques, you will be playing at a level beyond anything you have ever imagined.

ABOUT THE AUTHOR

Richard Behrens (New Mexico) is Grand Master, Tenth Degree
Black Belt of the esoteric martial art of Torishimaru Aiki Jutsu.
He is also the author of *The Lost Scrolls of King Solomon* and
Teachings of a Grand Master.

TO WRITE TO THE AUTHOR

If you wish to contact the author or would like more information about this book, please write to:

Richard Behrens
C/o Llewellyn Worldwide
P.O. Box 64383, Dept. K061-2
St. Paul, MN 55164-0383, U.S.A.

Please enclose a self-addressed stamped envelope for reply,
or $1.00 to cover costs. If outside U.S.A., enclose international
postal reply coupon.

Applying the Teachings of Martial Arts

Golf

• The Winner's Way •

Grand Master **RICHARD BEHRENS**

1999
Llewellyn Publications
St. Paul, Minnesota 55164-0383

FIRST EDITION
First Printing, 1999

Cover design: Michael David Matheny
Cover photo: Image copyright ©1998 PhotoDisc, Inc.
Interior illustrations: William Cannon
Book design and editing: Michael Maupin

Library of Congress Cataloging-in-Publication Data
Behrens, Richard, 1946 –
Golf : the winners way / Richard Behrens. — 1st ed.
p.   cm.
Includes bibliographical references and index.
At head of title: Applying the teachings of martial arts.
ISBN 1-56718-061-2
1. Golf—Psychological aspects. 2. Martial arts. I. Title.
II. Title: Applying the teachings of martial arts.
GV979.P75B45 1999
796.352′3—dc21
98-54745
CIP

Llewellyn Publications
A Division of Llewellyn Worldwide, Ltd.
P.O. Box 64383, Dept. K061-2
St. Paul, MN 55164-0383, U.S.A.

 Printed in the United States of America on recycled paper.

To God, my wife Sandra,
and to all those golfers around the world
who have waited so patiently for this book.

CONTENTS

Earth • Power Principle on the Back Swing: Yield and Return • Power Principle on the Down and Through Swing: The 30–70% Acceleration Principle • Power Principle at the Point of Impact: Club Face Alignment • The "Void-Through-Void" Principle • The "Nothing to Do" Principle • Breathing

CHAPTER 6
Achieving "The Zone" / 93

The "Zone"—What is It? • How to Access the Zone in Three Steps • Step 1: Putting Everything Down • Step 2: Focus • The Heart Sephira Technique • The 60-Second Meditation • Step 3: Just Doing

CHAPTER 7
Playing the Fairway / 111

Sensing the Course—the Pull of the Fairway • Playing the Wind • The Grip • Ball Position • Driving • Pitching • Chipping • Bunker Play • Trouble Shots

FOREWORD

WHEN I FIRST learned that Grand Master Richard Behrens had finally agreed to write a book on golf, I was elated. In fact, I pleaded with him for the opportunity to write the introduction to such an enlightening work, on a subject so dear to the hearts of tens of millions of people.

When I, and others, first approached Master Behrens with the idea that he write a book on golf, he declined our suggestion. We were disappointed, yes, but not disheartened. Fortunately, however, with a great deal of patient urging from me and various other golf enthusiasts around the country, he changed his mind and had decided to write this book. The publication of this book has us all looking forward with great anticipation to the enormous positive changes that his revolutionary principles will make in the golf games of millions of men and women, not only here in the United States, but throughout the world. I, and the others who have experienced these principles at work in their games, are agreed, unanimously, that this book will change the way the game of golf is played forever.

I have played golf at virtually every conceivable level, from a weekend hacker to a scratch tournament player. When I was playing tournaments, I felt I had an advanced grasp on the game. That is, until I sat down with Master Behrens and asked him about his concept of the mind, as it pertained to the game of golf.

After speaking to Master Behrens, I was both astonished and amazed at his vast wealth of knowledge in this area and realized just how primitive the "modern" concepts of relaxation, power, and accuracy being taught to golfers today actually are. Master's personal insights, gained through his meditations, and his deep rooted understanding of the machinations of the human mind seem to uniquely combine to transcend any topic, and golf proved to be no exception. "Good golf is all in the mind," Master said. He also told me that a golfer with sound mechanics, coupled with even a cursory understanding of his principles and techniques, would cause that player's game to enter a "New

Dimension." Possibly, the most important point that he stressed was, that the golfer's own lower mind, and how he perceives the situations he finds himself in on the course are the major reasons he suffers with unsatisfactory play.

My game improved so dramatically, and so quickly after applying the principles that he mapped out for me during that first conversation and other subsequent discussions, that it was nothing less than amazing, miraculous. I started to hit the ball one to two clubs longer with the irons, and thirty yards longer with the driver. "Not bad," I thought, but there was more. The improvements, also, filtered into every other area of my game, as well. I enjoyed greater accuracy both off the tee and from the fairway, hit more green in regulation, and lowered my average number of putts per round. Suddenly, golf was fun again!

When I discussed the value of these principles with others, we collectively presented our case to Master Behrens, explaining to him that every golfer needs to be exposed to these principles. To test the validity of his principles and techniques, he agreed to teach them to an established golf professional, and so we sought out the local PGA Chapter Teacher of the Year, Steven Underill. Who better then the best teacher in the area to experiment with? Underill, at that time, had thought his game was "maxed" out, but after meeting and working with Master on just a few principles, he started to appreciate what those principles would mean to the golfing community on an international scale. During the first lesson alone, Underill began to experience an immediate increase in his distance and enjoyed a new found control over his putting. Astounded, he pursued a course of study with Master Behrens spanning several years.

Soon, word spread in the golf world and Master Behrens was approached by various mini-tour pros, teaching pros, senior PGA pros, as well as several LPGA and PGA touring professionals. Because of a hectic schedule, he couldn't meet with all of them. You see at the time, Master Behrens was not only helping golfers, but he was also working with several NBA players, Olympic power lifters, Olympic swimmers, NFL players, and teaching the martial art of Torishimaru Aiki Jutsu, as well. As always, Master Behrens stressed that the lower mind is the one thing that all his students shared in common, regardless of their sport, and by teaching them to control their lower minds and tap into their "hidden" powers, all of them, without exception, experienced dramatic improvements in their particular sport.

Master Behrens' golf instruction is a unique bridge spanning physical golf technique, and the sometimes diffuse mental discipline of the game. On the physical side, techniques such as "Oneness with the Earth" generate an astoundingly solid sense of balance, which allows you to not only consistently achieve a proper impact position, but it also frees you to transfer your weight through the swing, and generate enormous club head speed as well. When a golfer is "One with the Earth," the body is allowed to remain kinetic throughout the swing. This foundation, coupled with the "30-70% Acceleration Principle" is guaranteed to increase your driving distance. After all, there is not a golfer alive who would not like to finally out-drive that one golf buddy who always sails it by him off the tee! Then there is the principle of "Turning the Club," or actually "turning your strength" at the top of your back-swing. This principle is paramount in marrying your back swing to your through-swing, and this, in conjunction with the "30-70% Acceleration Principle" when supported by a stance that is "One with the Earth," completes a "basic" equation of how to hit the ball further. This is just one example to illustrate how Master Behrens' physical principles work together in a logical order to bring about positive results.

Strangely, the mental aspect of the game is something that seems to elude most golfers, both amateurs and professionals alike. Not so surprisingly, this is the very area where Master Behrens' golf teachings truly excel and his genius is most evident. How many of you have talked yourself out of executing a shot that is well within your ability to make, or have carried anger with you from a poor hole throughout the rest of your game, effectively destroying a potentially good round of golf? Well, Master's uncanny ability to get a golfer to "live in the moment," or play one shot at a time, teaches you to "Put the Geisha Down" and get on with your round. This allows you to let go of harmful emotional baggage and truly enjoy the challenge of each shot you encounter while on the golf course. Then there is Master Behrens' extraordinary "Heart Sephira Technique," and his lesson of "Playing The 'Hole' Game." The Heart Sephira Technique, for example, is perhaps the most unique meditation and power-engendering technique in the world, and is specifically designed for the competing athlete and of enormous importance to the serious golfer. The principle of "Playing The 'Hole' Game," releases the pressure of attempting to complete a great score over the course of eighteen holes, or trying to follow a good nine-hole score with an even better one. These are burdens that golfers carry around with them for no reason, and are often the cause of great strife to a player who, after all, is supposed to be enjoying a relaxing day of golf in the sun.

This book is the gift that you owe to both yourself and your game. You should cherish it because it will allow you to finally enjoy and prosper in the game you love so well. Naturally, all I can do is mention in this introduction just a few excellent examples of what treasures await you. Take the time to understand each principle so that you can successfully incorporate them into your game.

My final testimony to the value of these principles, unfortunately, came at my own expense. You see, two years ago I herniated three discs in my lower back. Needless to say, this was not very good for my golf game, but after two years of treatment, recovery, and physical therapy, including more crunches than I can count, I received the "okay" from my doctor to start playing golf again. Immediately, I started to work with Master Behrens' principles, and my second round of golf after two years on injured reserve was a seventy-three . . ."Thank you, Master Behrens!"

To the rest of the golfing world, pros and amateurs alike, you are in for a real treat. Even if you incorporate only one of Master Behrens' principles into your game, you will notice an immediate improvement in your scores. Read, learn, and enjoy!

Fairways and greens!
STEVEN BROWNER
FOURTH DEGREE BLACK BELT,
TORISHIMARU AIKI JUTSU

PREFACE

WHEN FIRST ASKED to write this book, I declined the suggestion out-of-hand and dismissed the whole idea. When professional golfers came to me for help with their games, I would help them, yes, but shunned the notoriety that is so often produced by such a relationship with those in the public spotlight. Then, one day, I happened to be in a bookstore and, out of curiosity, perused the large number of golf books they had in their sports section.

For the most part, I found that they were well written by authors I had no doubt were leaders in their field. What I also noticed, however, was that they were all saying basically the same thing and that the only real difference between them were the author's name, the thickness of the book, publisher, and color of the book jackets. The more I looked through these books, the more I realized the need a golfer would have of the techniques and principles that I have used to quietly help a number of professional golfers achieve their desired goals.

Some of my students, with mischievous grins on their faces, have privately called my system "Behrens' golf," while others have called it a unique and well-structured system of "Twenty-first century golf." Whether they called it "Behrens'" golf or "Twenty-first century" golf, the point is that they all agreed that it not only works, but has truly added a new dimension to both their games and their careers. Like them, all that is required of you in order to improve your game beyond your wildest expectations is trust, understanding, and employment of the techniques and principles that I offer you in this book. Simply apply them to the preexisting, fundamentally sound, golfing techniques taught to you by your PGA Pro.

Regardless of how new or odd the techniques and principles may seem, I guarantee you that if you trust them and use them, you will be pleasantly surprised at the results. It is my contention that there is not a golfer in the world, regardless of how many years he or she has been playing, or what competitive heights they have achieved, whether amateur or professional, whose game will not improve if they use the techniques and principles contained in this book.

Of this, I have no doubts. Trust, learn, and employ these techniques and principles. You will not be sorry. You have my personal guarantee.

Yours in golf,
GRAND MASTER RICHARD BEHRENS

USING THIS BOOK

YOU WILL FIND as you read this book that many new concepts of strength, power and accuracy are introduced to you. Take the time to read what is presented here very carefully, and do not be afraid to reread those sections you have difficulty understanding. Each new concept, when used in your golf game, will change your game for the better. It is not necessary that you master all the techniques and principles in the book in order for you to clearly see a positive difference in your game.

Naturally, you will find that there are techniques and principles that you will pick up very quickly, and that there are those that will take time to both understand and master. This is the way of things. After all, it is a new and exciting dimension in golf that you are embarking on.

Read through the entire book once, and then you may reread the particular principles and techniques you want to introduce into your game first. Learn one or two principles or techniques at a time. Introduce them into your game, and you will happily find that your golf game will improve the very first day out.

By the time all the principles and techniques in this book are part of your game, you will be playing golf at a level well beyond anything you could have imagined.

CHAPTER 1

Some Basics

I HAVEN'T THE slightest doubt that a great many of the principles and techniques that I present in this book are going to be new to you. This, of course, will make some demands on you, but I promise you that if you apply these principles and techniques, your golf scores will improve beyond your wildest expectations. There is, however, a reasonable price that you will have to pay in order to succeed, and that price is to keep an open mind.

Keeping an Open Mind

Listen! There once was a man who wanted to study Zen. He studied every piece of literature that he could find on the subject. One day he appeared at a local Zen Master's house and after explaining to the Master that he wanted to learn Zen was invited in. Well, from the time he stepped through the door, all he did was talk about Zen. "Zen is this," he would say. "Zen is that!" The man was like an unstoppable chatterbox, telling the Master unceasingly everything he knew about Zen.

When the Master's servant brought in a tray of tea, the Master asked the man to sit down at the table. The Master then dismissed his servant, indicating that the Master, himself, would be serving the tea. Standing up, the Master walked over to his guest and slowly started to pour tea into his guest's cup. The Master poured and poured. The tea cup filled up, and began to overflow onto the table and onto his guest's lap. The man jumped up in pain, screaming for the Master to stopped pouring the tea. The shaken man said "Master, stop pouring the tea, the cup is full and you can't get any more tea into it!"

"Just so!" serenely replied the Master. "Look and see how full the tea cup of your mind is. You came here to learn about Zen, and yet, you brought with you so many of your own ideas, such a full mind, that I cannot possibly put any of the wisdom and knowledge that I have to teach you into it. If you want me to teach you, you must first bring me an empty teacup!"

Do you understand? You are reading this book in an attempt to improve your golf game. If you are reading this book with a "teacup" that is already full of "tea," how can you learn properly? In fact, how can you learn *anything*? I promise you, that if you bring me an "empty teacup" you will learn a great deal and it will be evident, not only in your scores, but in a new-found enjoyment of the game. This is, realistically, the only way to learn.

The Correct Way to Look at the Game

In the martial arts, we never look for results. We learn, sometimes painfully, that if we execute our techniques correctly, positive results will occur automatically. In golf, on the other hand, I find it very surprising that most golfers do just the opposite. They are so preoccupied with results that they sacrifice their technique. This way of thinking, this way of playing, of course, will almost invariably end poorly. We say that "a man who is always looking at the horizon, trips over things lying at his feet." In golf, you must not preoccupy yourself with final results while you are executing your techniques and employing your principles, you must learn to "do what you are doing, in the moment that you are doing them!"

Play the 'Hole' Game, Not the Whole Game

Most golfers, with few exceptions, see the game of golf in the context of an entire round, not realizing that a round of golf is really composed of eighteen separate and quite individual games. That's right, *eighteen separate games.*

Each hole is unique to itself, and presents to the golfer new and exciting demands, totally separate from all the other holes. Each hole has a beginning (the tee-shot) and a definitive ending (the final putt). Once the ball drops into the cup, that particular "game" is over, and you then move on to a new "game," a new hole, with a new beginning and a stimulating set of challenges.

Each hole or "new game" must be understood to consist of several strokes, and each stroke, in turn, must again, be looked at as a separate and individual "game." That "game" is, to take the ball from point "A" and, as *skillfully* as you can, move it to point "B." That is the ultimate challenge, the ultimate game. It is taking the ball one stroke at a time from the tee to the cup.

You must have a clear understanding that each hole is presenting you with a challenge. Each hole is saying to you "I dare you! I challenge you! I am a par three (or a par four or par five). If you par me, you win, if you bogey, I win; if you birdie, you win and embarrass me; if you eagle, you win and embarrass the people who designed me." That's the game, and you get to play eighteen of these games during each and every round. Look at the game this way, and you will be looking at the game correctly. It will not only make each round more fun, but will offer you rewards that will be reflected in your final score.

Who is Your Opponent, Anyway?

Over the years, I've heard statements from numerous tour players that would send chills down the spine of any accomplished martial artist. What were they saying? "I'm outclassed by this field, I don't stand a chance," "So and so showed up; she always beats me," or "Playing on television makes be nervous, I hope the other players don't make me look too bad." Statements like this tell me that the person who made them doesn't really understand who his or her opponent actually is. They mistakenly think that their opponents are the other players. This couldn't be further from the truth.

The fact is a golfer's opponent is not another player at all, it is *the golf course itself.* This is true in both stroke play and match play, as well. In stroke play, the object is to shoot the lowest score possible. In match play, your opponent's decisions often dictate the play, but if you play the golf course as I have suggested, a par, and most certainly a birdie will win you the hole almost all the time. Think about it! What the other players do has absolutely nothing to do with your score. That is, unless you plan on winning by default, hoping that if you finish your round with a stroke count of 120, everyone else will finish with a stroke count of 130 or more. Ouch! That would be like a martial artist having to defend himself during a very serious street attack by hoping that the attacker or attackers will all have heart-attacks and die of natural causes before any contact is made. The odds of that happening lie well beyond the realm of one's imagination. Your score is ultimately determined by what you do, not by what they do, and what you do is determined by the numerous rigors and challenges presented to you by each particular hole. Your "job" is to play against the hole, one perfect stroke at a time. Let the other players carry the burden of worrying about you.

I always tell tour players never to look at the leader board during the round. If you do and you are leading, you are apt to fall into complacency. If you are behind, you are apt to give up, thinking that you are too far behind, or you may press too hard to make up ground and suffer from self-imposed pressures and tensions. I remind players that the game of golf is only one perfect stroke at a time, and their only opponent is the golf course, not the other players.

Learning is Fun, Practice is Boring

In golf, as in most endeavors, learning is always fun. It is fun learning how to swing the club, to tee off, to putt, to play the game, but practicing can often become boring and tedious. Why? Because it is repetitious. Professionals, at least the successful ones, understand the need to practice, to spend countless hours at the driving range or on the practice green. Like everyone else, of course, they would rather spend their time playing a round of golf than stand in one place hitting a thousand buckets of balls, but they know that practice is one of the necessities of life. Amateurs, with some exceptions, generally, get bored very quickly during practice and most merely use the driving range and practice green as mere warm-up exercises, preludes to a round of golf.

The truth is: practice *is* boring! That is, it is boring the way an average golfer practices. You can change that. You can make practicing more interesting, more fun. How? It's all in how you look at it.

try this . . . The next time you go out to the driving range, play a round of golf. That is, play a par four on the range by driving your ball to a distant pin and then, depending how far from the pin your ball lands, change clubs and hit your approach shot to the green on a closer pin, approximating the distance. Take this practice a step further by using this exercise to prepare for an upcoming match or tournament by actually playing the golf course on your home driving range. Visualize each hole. For example, if Hole #1 is a par four that requires a hard hook off the tee, then pick a target and hit that first tee shot by hooking it to the flag. You can use this technique to play the entire game from tee to green for eighteen holes. If you do this you are "killing several birds with the same stone." First, you will be taking away the sense of tedium by replacing consecutive drives with various shorter strokes and different clubs. Secondly, you will have a sense of actually playing a hole. Thirdly, and certainly not least, it will bring you a real sense of accomplishment that will, in turn, make practicing much more agreeable to you and you will look forward to practicing more often.

The "Safe" Game

Many golfers, including a great many touring professionals, play what I call a "safe" game. That is, they simply refuse to take chances during their games, and in so doing, miss numerous opportunities for low stroke counts and victory. I have watched it happen over and over again. I have seen many a victory sacrificed for the sake of safety and, more often than not, for the mere "illusion" of safety.

It is no great secret that one of the big allures of the game is the challenge that the course presents to the golfer and, bearing this in mind, I find it more than just a little strange that most golfers are more than willing to accept the small challenges, yet buckle under the pressures presented to them by the larger ones. Anyone wanting to improve their scores must be willing to take those big chances, especially if they are touring professionals and are involved in tournaments where every stroke they save moves them up the leader board; where every stroke they save translates into higher tournament earnings.

There are predominantly two areas where you must take those chances. The first are the realistically manageable hazards. Many a golfer, for example, even if they have the power to cross a particular water hazard, will sacrifice a stroke and navigate around it, or if there is a dog-leg to the left with a stand of trees in the way, they will stroke around the trees rather than taking the chance and firing the shot over them, resulting in optimum position in the fairway for an approach shot onto the green. The second area is on the green. Here, on manageable longer putts, intimidated golfers opt to lag the ball to the hole instead of going for the money. Think about this: If you lag the ball to the hole for each of the eighteen holes, you just sacrificed eighteen strokes. Can your game really afford that?

Overcoming the Safe Game

In order to overcome the Safe Game Syndrome, you must place yourself in a "sudden death" mode. That is, every shot you take must be played as if the entire game depended on it. In the martial arts, every individual strike we make in combat must be a meaningful strike; there can be no wasted effort when one's life is at stake. Similarly, in golf every stroke must be purposeful and decisive. When the golf course offers you a water hazard or a stand of trees in your way, and you know that you have the power to go over them, then you must go over them! You must go where angels fear to tread, undaunted by the challenges of the course. Besides, shaving strokes off your final stroke count, you will find golf more stimulating, more fun, and in the cases involving monetary rewards, much more profitable.

Again, on the green you must always play in the "sudden death" mode. Every putt must be played as a win or lose stroke. Never lag the ball to play a safe game. Every putt must be calculated to drop that ball into the cup. Of course, you should be mindful of your speed and power, but you must go for the "gold." While working with touring pros I have found, at times, a very strange mind-set when it comes to lagging the ball on the green. With all their years of experience, with all their acquired skills, on longer putts they consciously try just to place the ball near the cup rather than into the cup. It may seem safe, but it will always cost strokes in the long run. You won't find them very often on top of the leader board. At best, you will find them consistently in the middle or lower part of the pack. Remember, lag the ball once on each green and you are amassing as many as eighteen "extra" strokes. Ouch!

The Safety of Mediocrity

One time I was asked to help a certain LPGA touring pro with her game. It seems that in over fourteen years on the tour, she had never won a title, she never had a victory. She was certainly a skillful player and had many of the attributes that would make a champion, but what held her back was what I call "the safety of mediocrity." She had the status of a tour player, the golfing skills of a tour player, but for some reason, even unknown to her, she lacked the victories. After watching her play two rounds of golf in competition I discovered her problem. Deep inside her was the fear that if she actually did win a big event it would put an inordinate amount of pressure on her to continue winning titles. She didn't want that kind of pressure, so she would follow excellent rounds of golf with mediocre rounds of golf, keeping her constantly in the middle of the pack. Yes, it kept her safe, but it also kept her from victories, titles, and large checks. I worked with her on this for an entire weekend and a month later she not only won a prestigious victory, but did so while tying the tournament record. However, she is not alone. There are many excellent players who have this same problem. The real pressure that a player faces doesn't come from the outside, but from the inside. It is the pressure he places on himself, created and perpetuated by his own imagination. This may sound odd to you, but anyone who plays golf for a living must be *willing to accept victory,* or if they can't, they should either get help, or get out of the game.

Trimming the Scores

Increasing your power will mean longer drives and longer fairway shots. Naturally, you won't notice a big difference on par three holes, but on your par four and par five holes an increase in power will translate into saving many strokes over the course of the game. That is, an increase in power of forty to fifty yards, means that many of your approach shots will be struck with one of your scoring clubs (eight-iron through sand wedge) into par four holes, while many of the par five holes will be reachable in two strokes, and some even with a mid-to-long iron. More green hits mean less strokes counted on the scorecard.

Let's say that over the course of the round you save nine strokes just because you have applied all the principles of power that you find in this book. You will agree that nine strokes is a lot. This, of course, holds, not only for the amateur, but for the professional who believes that his power has peaked-out long ago.

For example, using the Sudden Death Principle will save you many strokes on the green. Instead of lagging the ball and voluntarily piling up strokes, you will be shaving those strokes off your final score. If you use the Sudden Death Principle along with the Principles for Putting Accuracy, you can conservatively save yourself an estimated nine strokes there.

Utilizing these principles and techniques, mid-to-high handicap amateurs stand an excellent chance of decreasing each round by at least eighteen strokes, while touring pros and low handicap amateurs can use them and elevate their games to the next level. Think about it. Wouldn't golf be sweet!

The Need to Win

Certainly, just about everyone who enters a competition does so with the desire to win. This is healthy and natural, but when that desire to win becomes a "need" to win, things change. The need to win often forces us to do things that are against our personal moral standards. "Need" is corrupting and blinding! It prompts us to cheat and lie about our scores, has us changing the position of our ball when we think that no one is looking, and has us "over-trying" on the links. The need to win drives our minds into the future and away from the matter at hand, and is to be assiduously avoided.

You should never have the "need" to win. Just play your game. Cheating doesn't improve your skills, it merely improves the illusion of your skills when presented to others. It will also cloud any improvement you may develop in your game. Honesty should be part of your game. If you fire a round of 95, that's fine; a round of 80, that's fine; a round of 66 that's fine; a round of 105, that's fine too. There can be no accurate barometer of your improvement if the need to win, the need to impress others, or the need to reduce embarrassment, corrupts both your morals and your judgment.

What Happened to the Fun?

Without exception, everyone who ever earnestly took up the game of golf did so because they thought it would be fun. When they realized that it actually *was* fun, they stayed with it. Didn't you? Is it still fun? If it isn't, what happened? Perhaps all the fun was replaced by frustration, anger, and a general sense of hopelessness. Whether you are a one-day-a-week golfer, or play the game for a living and somehow have lost contact with the "fun" aspect of the game, you have to realize that it isn't the game that changed, something deep inside of "you" has changed.

The cure is really very simple. If you are an amateur or "Sunday" golfer, don't care so much. There you are in the great outdoors, in the fresh air and sunshine, getting exercise. There are no job pressures, no domestic or monetary problems at the golf course, unless you bring them with you. Leave them home, or at the office, and for a few hours, at least, be problemless.

If you are a professional golfer, what happened to the fun? Think back to when you first started your career, the excitement, the promise of a bright and rewarding future. What changed? Did you "run out of future?" As long as you have a tournament to play next week you have a future. There you are, doing what you love to do and actually getting paid for it. Not many people in life have that kind of opportunity. Take the time to "stroll down memory lane" and reflect a little bit on the game and your career, the fun will return. When it does so, your attitude will change and your career will renew itself. That renewal will be reflected in both your status and your pocket.

CHAPTER 2

Warm-Up and Stretching

IF YOU ARE a professional or a seasoned amateur golfer then you should already know the value in warm-up and stretching exercises. If you are a beginning golfer, or a seasoned golfer who either doesn't know the enormous value of warm-up and stretching exercises (or simply chooses to ignore them), then you should closely read the following and then decide whether or not to include them as an intricate part of your game.

The following is a list not only of the benefits to warm-up and stretching exercises, but also the detriments of not employing them, as well as the reasons why many golfers avoid them.

Benefits of Warm-Up and Stretching

- Warming up and stretching exercises greatly reduce the possibility of injury during your golf game.

- Warming up and stretching keeps the muscles of the body relaxed, which will translate into more power and greater distances for your drives and fairway shots.

- The muscles of the body are affected by a number of conditions, some internal and some external. Nervousness, lack of proper rest, and personal as well as business problems, are examples of internal conditions that affect the body's muscles. Warming up and stretching the body reduces the stress that cause tense muscles from these internal conditions. External conditions such as temperature and humidity also affect the body's muscles. For example, when the weather is chilly or cold, your muscles will tighten, and this will negatively affect your game.

- Consistency is a very important attribute in any sport, but is particularly important in the game of golf. Warming up and stretching before each round will keep the muscles of the body "consistently" relaxed, and this will translate into a consistent swing with consistent results.

- Most golfers enjoy the game because of the physical exercise and the health benefits they derive from it.

Warming up and stretching, if included as part of your game, will only enhance those physical and health benefits.

Detriments to Not Warming Up and Stretching

- Tense muscles are the leading cause of injury in golf, and so you are placing your physical well-being in jeopardy by not warming up and stretching.

- The body and the mind are not two things. That is, what affects one, affects the other. If the mind is tense, then the body will be tense, and, conversely, if the body is tense, the mind will become tense. A tense mind and a tense body, as I am sure you already know, not only affects your skill level, but actually turns your game into "work," consequently taking all the enjoyment out of it.

- Tense muscles greatly reduce your strength as I will explain in greater detail later in the book.

Why Many Golfers Avoid Warm-Up and Stretching

Note: Be honest with yourself when you read this list. Without honesty there is no progress.

- You didn't know that golfers should warm up and stretch before play.

- You are simply lazy, and think that just bending down to put the tee in the ground is more than enough warming up and stretching to get you through the day. If this is you, and you want to improve both your game and your health, then you should reconsider and change.

- You are afraid that if your golfing buddies see you warming up and stretching, they will decrease your handicap, and you'll wind-up having to buy the drinks at the nineteenth hole.

- You think that the more strokes you take during a game, the more exercise you will get, and the greater the health benefits you will receive. If this is you, then you must take the time and learn more about the game.

Things to Remember When Doing these Exercises

- Find a quiet place for warming up and stretching, one free of disturbance and distraction. You can, if you like, perform these exercises at home, just before leaving for the golf course.

- There should be no strain or pain during the execution of any of these exercises. If doing these exercises, you feel any pain at all, it means that you have gone too far. Ease up.

- "Extreme" position means that point in your stretching that lies just before you experience pain. There should never be any pain associated with these exercises.

- Just *do* the exercises! That is, while you are doing the exercises you should not have anything else on your mind. You shouldn't, for example, be thinking of your golf game, your wife's sister's niece's French poodle's doghouse current renovation, or the absurdly high retail price of a good pair of snow skis for your blindfolded run down the windward side of

Mount Everest next winter. You must keep your mind on what you are doing in the moment that you are doing it.

- Never be in a rush to finish any of the exercises. Take your time and try to feel what is happening to both your body and your mind during their execution.

The Bend Exercise

Purpose: To stretch and exercise the arms, shoulders, stomach, and upper and lower back muscles.

Comments: This exercise must be executed very slowly. Don't rush to complete it.

Technique:
1. Standing with both feet together, raise both hands, palms upward, in front of you until they are shoulder high.

2. Turn both palms forward and then "push" them slowly to full extension.

3. Very slowly swing your arms to the rear and clasp both of your hands (see Figure 2A).

FIGURE 2A:

*The Bend Exercise
(Step 3)*

4. Extend your clasped hands and arms behind you as you slowly and gently bend backwards at the waist. When you reach the limit of your backward bend, hold the position for a count of ten (Figure 2B).

5. Bend forward at the waist until you reach the limit of the bend, and hold the position for a count of ten (Figure 2C).

6. Unclasp your hands and relax your arms as you slowly straighten into the original standing position. Repeat this exercise three times.

One-Leg Stretch Exercise (for Balance)

Purpose: To promote balance, and to stretch and exercise the rectus femoris muscles of the thighs.

Comments: This is a balance exercise. In the beginning you may feel very awkward and fall off-balance. In time you will achieve balance and will fall over less and less frequently. Eventually, you will be able to maintain your balance without effort. Don't become discouraged.

FIGURE 2D:

One-Leg Stretch Exercise

Technique:

1. Standing with both feet together, bend your right leg backwards at your knee and secure your foot with your right hand pulling slightly upward.

2. Simultaneously, slowly stretch your left arm upward toward the ceiling, palm upward (Figure 2D, page 31).

3. Hold this extreme position for a count of ten and then reverse the exercise changing arms and legs. Repeat this exercise three times.

Inner Thigh Stretch Exercise

Purpose: To stretch and exercise the muscles of the knee and inner thighs, as well as to stretch out the hamstring muscles.

Comments: Do not rush through this exercise. Hold the extreme position for a full count of fifteen.

Technique:

1. Sitting on the floor, place the soles of your feet together and secure them with both hands (Figure 2E).

FIGURE 2E:

Inner Thigh Stretch Exercise

2. Pull them in as close to your body as is comfortable.

3. Slowly lower your knees until they reach their limit of movement. Hold this extreme position for a count of fifteen and then relax.

4. Without changing position, lower your knees again for another count of fifteen. Repeat a third time for a total of three sets.

The Cobra Exercise

Purpose: To stretch and exercise the muscles of the abdomen, neck, shoulders, chest, and back.

Comments: Do this exercise very slowly. Refer to the illustrations when necessary to make sure you are doing it correctly. At the end of each set of this exercise, rest, allowing your entire body to go limp. You will experience a great feeling of relaxation.

Technique:
1. Lie on your stomach with your arms at your side and with the left side of your face resting on the floor. Allow your body to relax (Figure 2F).

FIGURE 2F:

The Cobra Exercise (Step 1)

FIGURE 2G:

The Cobra Exercise (Step 2)

FIGURE 2H:
The Cobra Exercise (Step 3)

2. Very slowly turn your head until you are facing the floor, and then raise it in an attempt to look toward the ceiling, slowly stretching your head, neck, shoulders and upper torso off the floor in the process without using your hands, which are still at your side, to aid you (Figure 2G, page 35).

3. Slowly and gently, in an outward arc, bring your hands to a position on the floor just below and in line with your chin. Hands should be turned in, with your fingers pointing toward each other (Figures 2H and 2I).

4. Now, with your hands, push gently upward arching your head, neck, and back (Figure 2J).

FIGURE 2I:
The Cobra Exercise (Step 3)

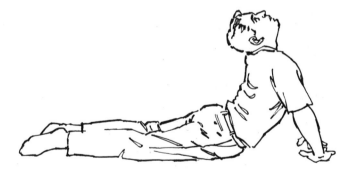

FIGURE 2J:
The Cobra Exercise (Step 4)

5. When you reach the point of maximum stretch, hold the position for a count of ten.

6. Slowly begin to lower yourself reversing the procedure.

7. When your shoulders and torso reach approximately halfway, then slowly, in an outward arc, move your hand back to your sides.

8. Then very slowly lower your head, neck, and shoulders toward the floor.

9. As your head nears the floor, slowly turn it to the left and rest the left side of your head on the floor as in the original position.

This exercise should be done three times.

Lateral Stretching Exercise

Purpose: To both stretch and revitalize muscle groups that golfers employ during the execution of their swing, preventing golf-related injuries to those muscles.

Comments: This is an extremely important exercise for a golfer, since it stretches the muscles used during the swing. Do not skip this exercise.

Technique:

1. Stand with your feet at shoulders' width apart, your arms at your sides.

2. Relax and raise both your arms outward, and laterally from your body until they are both parallel to the floor.

3. Now, turn your palms so that they are facing outward and slowly stretch your arms "leading" with the base of the palms of your hands. If this is done correctly you will feel your wrist and forearm muscles begin to stretch. Hold this extreme position for a count of ten.

4. Now, twist your torso at the waist as far as you can go toward your right and hold the extreme position for a count of ten (Figure 2K, page 40).

FIGURE 2K:
Lateral Stretching Exercise

5. Then, reverse it and twist to your left, holding that extreme position, also, for a count of ten.

6. Then, simply untwist and come to rest with both of your hands at your side.

7. Do three sets of this exercise.

Dead Man's Pose Exercise

Purpose: To exercise and relax not only major muscle groups but minor muscle groups as well. It promotes total relaxation.

Comments: This is the ultimate relaxation exercise. Its origins date back to antiquity. It is so relaxing, in fact, you may not want to get up for a while.

Techinque:

1. Lie on your back with your eyes closed, your head centered and your arms at your sides, with the palms of your hands turned upwards (Figure 2L, page 42).

2. Tense the muscles of both feet by curling your toes toward your heels and hold for a count of ten. Then relax them. Do the same thing by tensing all the muscles of both legs and hold for a count of ten

FIGURE 2L:
Dead Man's Pose Exercise (Step 1)

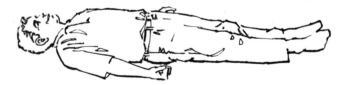

FIGURE 2M:
Dead Man's Pose Exercise (Steps 2, 3)

before relaxing them. You will follow the same procedure systematically for your stomach muscles, hands (clinched into fists), arms, chest, shoulders, neck, and facial muscles (Figure 2M).

3. Finally, after each set of muscles indicated above has been tensed and relaxed, you will proceed to then tense your entire body, all the muscles and hold that tense position for a count of twenty. Then relax. Lie for a minute or two with your eyes closed and simply "float." Enter the relaxation; feel the relaxation!

CHAPTER 3

Mind Basics

GOLF, AS YOU may already know, is not just a physical sport, it is also a *mental* sport. In order to grasp the many concepts and techniques that I have developed over the years and have included in this book, you must first come to understand the nature of the mind. This understanding will go a long way in your endeavors to improve your golf game.

The Nature of the Mind

Everyone has a lower mind and a higher mind. The lower mind may be thought of as a sort of limited cassette tape that begins to record everything from the time of conception. It is born with the body and ultimately dies with the body. It is the reasoning, hoping, fearing, dreaming, loving, hating part of you. It is insidious and capricious to a fault and is chiefly responsible for the ten thousand little miseries that a person suffers during his or her lifetime. It is highly fallible and predictably inconsistent.

Unless you are trained, this lower mind has been in control of not only your life, but in control of your golf game as well. If you have ever missed a simple putt, been afraid of a longer putt, succumbed to the pressures of competition, fired a brand new ball into a bottomless water hazard, or, in anger, bent an expensive club around a tree, then you can be sure the lower mind is responsible.

The lower mind, being loquacious to a fault, simply doesn't know when to be quiet. It is constantly chattering away. Ironically, you want everyone around you to be quiet when you are about to take your stroke, and out of respect they are-everyone is quiet, that is, except *you*. Your lower mind will simply not "shut up." It chatters away incessantly distracting you with all sorts of unwanted thoughts. Even when you order it to "keep quiet," it ignores you and continues its ten thousand little distractions (i.e., my wife, my car troubles, my business prospects, my cousin's friend's sister's French poodle's new haircut, etc.). An undisciplined lower mind is a golfer's greatest enemy. You can, in a way, think of the undisciplined lower mind as a broken radio, one without an on-off switch, and there you are strapped to a chair in front of it and forced to listen to whatever it plays. You can be sure that whatever it plays is going to break your concentration. This, of course, will inevitably translate into high stroke counts, frustration, and a growing dissatisfaction with your game.

The higher mind, on the other hand, is eternal and serene. It can be thought of as a cassette tape with unlimited recording capabilities. The significant feature of the higher mind when it comes to golf, or any sport for that matter, is its infallibility. It is unerringly accurate in everything it does, and is in fact simply incapable of making a mistake. Fear, anger, or frustration do not exist within the realm of the higher mind . . . only peace. Further, it has under its control a tremendous reservoir of power totally inaccessible by the limited abilities of the lower mind. It is the higher mind that an athlete uses when he or she is in the "zone." Imagine, if you will, how your game would improve if you could bring such a powerful, omnipotent, unerring ally under your direct control. If this is what you want, then read on, because the meditative techniques and golf principles that I present throughout this book are designed to help you do just that. Trust them; they will not fail you. You may be very pleasantly surprised at the results.

Natural Frequencies

Everyone has what I call a "Natural Operating Frequency." This is the operating frequency that is "natural" for a person when they are relatively stress-free. It can also be thought of as their "normal" operating frequency. When in this mode, everything appears normal to them, and sensory information is assimilated in a normal way. However, when stress is present, a person's "frequency" is altered, it is raised. When this occurs, trouble ensues. Sensory information seems to come in great deluges, thoughts become jumbled and difficult to deal with, and confusion dominates. This stress-born raise in frequency and sensory bombardment is ultimately reflected in one's physical performance.

The value of any meditation (i.e., The Heart Sephira Technique, The 60-Second Meditation, see pages 103–106) is that it reduces stress and thwarts "raised frequency;" it keeps your "operating" frequency low. You could say that the lower your operating frequency is, the lower your stroke count will be after the round. Bearing this in mind, you should encourage yourself to make meditation part of your game, especially, if you are one that must endure the rigors of competitive golf, whether you are an amateur or professional.

Tension — "The Silent Consistency Killer"

One of the great problems that a golfer faces on the course is tension. Tension is what I term "the silent consistency killer." Why, *silent* consistency killer? Because a golfer, more often than not, does not even know it is there. You must understand that the mind and the body are not unrelated, and that, what affects one, also, affects the other. When the mind is tense, the body is tense; when the mind is relaxed, the body is relaxed. I know that you understand this. However, what you need to appreciate is the fact that mind-induced tension in the body affects the muscles you use when you swing your club. The more tense your mind, the more your body muscles will contract, producing an inward pull toward your body. This inward pull will, literally, change your swing and affect, negatively, the flight of your ball. Since tension in the mind will vary, not only from day to day, but at various times during the course of a day, that variation will be reflected in your inconsistent ball flight, even during a single round of play.

Please understand that mental tension is not always apparent. In fact, you may even feel fine, and not even notice it, but it may be there lurking deep within the dark recesses of your mind, silently affecting your swing. Your swing may actually be perfect in all other respects, but the "silent consistency killer," tension, could have you making changes in your swing that are completely unnecessary and this, of course, will lead to a very unrewarding round of golf.

The key to removing this problem is meditation. The Heart Sephira Technique and the 60-Second Meditation explained in this book are, for example, two such techniques that you can use during the course of your game. They will ease both the apparent and non-apparent tensions existing in the mind, and this will translate into a uniform relaxation of the body, which will, in turn, create a more consistent swing. Never underestimate the value of the Heart Sephira Technique and the 60-Second Meditation; they are two of your keys to successfully eradicating tension from your golf game forever.

The Folly of Superstition

Many athletes, especially professional athletes, have an absurd, driving affinity toward superstitions. They carry lucky charms, four-leaf clovers, lucky coins, shrunken heads, and rabbit's feet of assorted sizes and colors. After all, how lucky can a rabbit's foot be, if the rabbit, who had four of them, is either dead or an incurable paraplegic and you have one of his "lucky" feet on a chain in your pocket? In fact, I've instructed athletes who have actually locked themselves into objects that the average person would throw away. For example, I instructed an NBA basketball star who could not play a basketball game without wearing his lucky sneakers. When I saw them, they looked as if they were disintegrating on his feet, in fact, he had tape on them in certain key areas just to extend their life and "his career" a little longer. Absurd? Of course. Athletes like this treat objects of superstition as the primary source of all their success. The question now arises, do you? Do you have some object of superstition that you depend on to get you through your game? If you do, then get rid of it, or find and join a local chapter of "Superstition Anonymous" and free yourself.

Perhaps, you think that Tuesdays are unlucky for you, or you refuse to enter a tournament on a month containing the letter "o" or, if you can't hear the sound of crickets chirping the night before a tournament that you are doomed to golfing oblivion. You must let go of these things. You must understand that your skills are acquired by your patient understanding and practice of the requirements of the game. Practicing your swing is preferable and more skill-producing than wearing your lucky socks, and practicing your putting is infinitely more preferable, practicable, and skill-producing than swinging a dead chicken over your head at a crossroads at midnight the night before a round of golf or a tournament. Practice *golf,* not magic!

Stop Painting Pictures

As you think, you make the world. Listen! One day, a man decided that he wanted to paint a picture of a dragon. Since he had never actually seen a real dragon in person, he decided to travel from village to village to find someone who had seen one. He searched the countryside for a week and could not find anyone who had actually seen a dragon. Undismayed, he decided to paint one anyway. He went back to his studio, set up his easel, took up his brushes and paints and began to paint what he thought was a dragon. When he was finished, he stepped back to see what he had painted. What he painted was so real, so frightening to him, that he threw his palette and brushes into the air and ran screaming in terror from the room.

Was this man wise or foolish? Foolish, of course! Why? Because, the dragon that he painted was nothing more than the product of his own imagination. He thought it up, painted it, and was frightened by his own creation. Do you paint pictures? I know many golfers who do. They paint pictures of all sorts of things. They paint pictures of record-breaking slices, hooks, bad lies, sand traps, water hazards, alligators on the sixteenth hole, lightning with their name on it, etc. All of these "painted pictures" are mind-created and negatively influence one's performance during a golf game. Even tour players with many years' experience—professionals who are supposed to have their games down pat—paint pictures that literally "drive" them right out of contention and large purses.

If you want to know when you are painting pictures, that is easy. One of the most salient warning signs to look for is the tell-tale "arbitrary" opinion. Basically, an arbitrary opinion is an opinion about an object, person, place, event, etc., that you blurt out either to yourself or to someone else without being asked. For example, you are in the process of addressing the ball when suddenly you say to yourself, "Boy, this is a tough hole!" or "My drives are terrible" or "I can't get the hang of this game!" or "I'm going to embarrass myself in front of everyone" or "I'll never be a good golfer," etc. These are arbitrary opinions. Who asked you anyway?

Arbitrary opinions are the "paints" that you use to paint, not only your golf game, but your world as well. If the paints you use are dark, then your game, attitudes, confidence, and world are going to be dark. Conversely, if your paints are bright, then what you see and experience will be bright. The problem is, that whether you are using bright hues or dark tones to paint your pictures, you are *still* painting pictures. Take your paints and brushes and toss them into the nearest "bottomless" water hazard.

You must assiduously and systematically get rid of all your arbitrary opinions, or you will be dooming yourself to a golf game fraught with anger, fear, frustration, insecurity, and a thousand other disagreeable emotions.

try this . . . In order to help you to help yourself get rid of your arbitrary opinions, try this little experiment. Keep a small notebook and pencil with you at all times during your round of golf, and should you come-up with an "arbitrary" opinion, place a check mark (✓) on the dated page. At the end of the round, see how many check marks you have accumulated. Compare it with the next round's check marks. Understand, there is no passing or failing. Be honest with yourself and place a check mark when appropriate. This little exercise will help you to monitor your lower mind. It will show you just how many times during the course of your golf game you take out your pigments and brushes and paint the world. By the way, if you just thought to yourself that this exercise is silly or stupid or even good or wonderful, then I've got you: you just produced an "arbitrary" opinion, so give yourself a check mark!

CHAPTER 4

Oneness

To me, there is really very little difference between a golf club and a sword. Both are swung and result in striking a target, and both require great skill in order to be truly effective. However, I've noticed both with the amateur and professional golfers I've worked with, the obvious lack of "oneness" they had with the club they were using. They each held the club as if it were something separate and apart from themselves. In swordsmanship this "separateness" can be fatal, while in "golfmanship" it can, and often is, a leading factor to poor scores and high handicaps.

As with the sword, someone who develops oneness with the club maintains an uncanny control over that club well beyond the ordinary. This "uncanny" control moves them into another class of golfer altogether. When Oneness is achieved, the club becomes an extension of your arm, an extension of yourself. I teach that the sword and the swordsman are not two. That is,

61

their individual spirits merge to form one united spirit with one immutable purpose: victory. Similarly in golf, I teach that the golfer and the golf club are not two, and that their spirits should merge toward one immutable purpose—great golf! The following three steps will help you achieve "oneness."

Step 1: Oneness with the Club

Resting the club head on the ground just behind the ball, while holding the club with your grip of choice, begin to follow your breath. To do this, imagine that the golf club you are holding is entirely hollow, like a straw (Figure 4A). First take a deep breath, allowing that breath to fill your entire body beginning at your feet, as if your body were completely hollow. Then, exhale very slowly (through your nose) and follow the path of your breath, mentally visualizing it as it travels up from your feet, through your hollow body, through your hollow arms, through the hollow club and out of the club head. When you inhale, you will reverse the procedure and draw your breath upwardly through the club head, up the hollow shaft, through your hollow arms, and allow that breath to fill your entire body.

FIGURE 4A:

Oneness with the Club

Step 2: Oneness with the Ball

Once you have developed oneness with the club, the next step is to become one with the ball. Actually, this is a very simple step, a mere extension of the first exercise.

Now that you have established "breathing" through the club, you will now apply it to the ball by simply extending that breath, so that when it leaves the club head it now extends to the ball. That is, as your breath leaves the club head, it will now pass through the ball so that we now have oneness developing between you, the club and the ball. Breathe in from the ball itself, through the club, through your hollow arms and into your hollow body, and then reversing the process, breathe out from your body, through your hollow arms, through the hollow club and into the ball (Figure 4B).

FIGURE 4B:

Oneness with the Ball

Step 3: Oneness with the Target

Once you have established Step 1 and Step 2, you are now ready to develop Oneness with the Target. What target? The hole, of course. In the martial arts we say that the "target and the arrow are one." In theory, to me, there is not much difference between placing an arrow in a small paper cup at a distance of one hundred yards, and putting a small ball in a four-inch hole in the ground. This step, even in the mere practice of it, will greatly improve your golf game. When mastered, you will be playing golf, in many respects, with the best of them. It will take you out of the realm of the "hacker-duffer" and move you up quite a few rungs on the golfing ladder of success or, if you are already a successful golfer, it will move you up to the next level of achievement. Again, it is an extension of the oneness exercises (Steps 1 and 2) you have just learned.

Once you understand and can apply Oneness with the Club and Oneness with the Ball, you simply extend your breath in a straight line to include the target or hole. This means that you will now be breathing in from the bottom of the hole, through the ball, through the golf club, through your "hollow" arms, and into your "hollow" body (Figure 4C).

FIGURE 4C:
Oneness with the Target

In exhaling, you will simply reverse the process. Exhaling through your "hollow" arms, through the "hollow" club, through the ball and into the target or hole. In order to be truly effective, you must be able to visualize your breath. That is, you must be able to "see" with your mind's eye the path that your breath is taking right to the target. Once you can see this, you are ready to hit the ball. You must never be in a rush to make your shot. Wait, however long it takes, to establish this visualization. Why? Because, this will establish the path that both your mind and spirit will take, and where your mind and spirit go, your ball will go.

In time, just before each shot, Oneness with the Target will take place automatically, without a conscious effort. It will become an intricate part of your game and give you "uncanny" control of your club and seemingly miraculous accuracy in the placement of the ball. Trust and practice these Oneness Principles. They will not fail you.

General Rules for All Three Steps

- Time permitting, practice the Oneness Techniques described above for a minimum of ten to fifteen minutes during your practice sessions, or before each round of golf.

- In executing each step, experience the feeling of what is taking place. Actually *feel* the breath as it travels from deep within the "hollowness" of your body through your arms, the club, the ball, and the hole, and back again.

- Make sure that the length of your inhalation or exhalation is coordinated with the visualization of your breath as it travels back and forth through the club, ball, and target. You should not run out of breath if your visualization is correct. However, if you do run out of breath, simply make the adjustment, and slow down your breathing.

CHAPTER 5

Developing True Power

WEIGHT TRAINING IN Torishimaru Aiki Jutsu is assiduously avoided. Those who practice weight training to develop "true" power are, invariably, doomed to failure. Why? Because weight training creates bulky, tense muscles that not only restrict required movement and slows one down, but actually *impedes* the development of true power. To understand how and why this happens, you must understand that whenever a muscle tenses, it contracts. This contraction translates as an inward pull towards your own body. When you are swinging a golf club, that swing is actually a movement away from your body. With tense muscles working toward your body, it follows that your muscles would then be working against you, impeding your movement and limiting the power of your swing.

Of course, this is why the meditation and relaxation exercises presented previously in this book are so important. When the mind is relaxed, the body's muscles are relaxed. This can be better understood by thinking of water flowing through a garden hose you hold in your hands. The water in this analogy represents strength flowing through your body. What would happen if you tightened your grip on the hose? That's right. By tightening your grip you would reduce its circumference and impede the flow of water. That is exactly what happens when you tense your muscles: they contract and reduce your flow of strength. In the martial arts, we call this marvelous esoteric strength, *Ki*. When mastered, this energy allows you to do some astounding things.

For example, in a live demonstration for television, I stood on one foot and held off twenty-two men lined-up one behind the other, who tried to push me over. I held them off with one hand and without any strain whatsoever. In this line-up there were some professional football players from the Miami Dolphins, Olympic gold medalist weight lifters, a couple of players from the Miami Heat and other assorted athletes. Astounding? Only to those who do not understand what "real" power is. In another demonstration that night, I allowed ten of the largest of those men to, simultaneously, attempt to lift me off the ground. I am only 150 pounds and yet they couldn't budge me. Why? Because they attempted to lift me with ordinary physical strength. They were at an extreme disadvantage. It was a poor match-up. I was demonstrating in both of these cases a principle that we in the martial arts call "Oneness with the Earth." I allowed the "strength" of the earth to flow through me; I "merged" with the earth. You can employ the following exercises and techniques in your golf game to give you that kind of "true" power.

Listen. Several years ago I met with Steve Underill, a PGA chapter Teacher of the Year, at a local country club to introduce to him some of my techniques and principles. Although he agreed to this meeting, he was not quite sure just what a Grand Master of a martial art would be able to do to help improve his game. He was convinced that his game had "peaked-out" years ago and that his power, because of his age, was steadily declining. Furthermore, he was sure that any improvement in his present game would be minor at best. He asked me just what I can do for his golf game. I smiled and said, "Suppose it were possible for me to add fifty yards to your drives and make you deadly accurate on the green?" He smiled a doubtful smile and asked how long it would take me to accomplish such a feat. I told him that if he would trust me and do exactly as I say, it would happen today. He decided to trust me. That day he added fifty yards to his drives. In fact, the yardage he used to carry using his driver, he was now carrying with his three wood.

Like Steve Underill, you must take a chance. You must put aside all of your current notions of strength, and trust me. If you do, you will be pleasantly surprised at the results. What do you have to lose?

Here are the three basic rules to remember to achieve distance:

Rule 1:
Go For Distance First, Not Accuracy

When you are practicing the power principles on the golf range, you should never be concerned initially with accuracy, only distance. When you are practicing your power principles, you can be sure that, within a very short period of time, accuracy will come automatically. Many golfers who attempt to increase their power, while simultaneously worrying about their accuracy, develop neither power nor accuracy. Here, you will find that if you trust your higher mind, your accuracy will come with surprising swiftness. In fact, if your "full swing" fundamentals are sound, your accuracy should not be affected at all when you use these new principles of power to increase the distance of your full shots.

Rule 2:
Everything Must Move Down Range

To increase your power, everything must move down range. That is, both your mind and body must move in a steady stream down the fairway. It is not a mere "intellectual understanding" of moving down range, but experienced as an actual sensation. In Chapter 7: Playing the Fairway, "Sensing the Course," you will learn how to feel the "draw" of the fairway. The "draw of the fairway," coupled with the oneness between yourself, the club, the ball, and the target, will give you the sensation of a "flow" of Ki, or power, down range. This is an inevitable experience, a natural product of the coupling of both "Oneness" and "The Draw of the Fairway," that will serve as a milestone in your personal evolution. You will know it when it happens. It will come over you as a positive revelation, and you won't be able to stop smiling for the rest of the day!

Rule 3:
Keep the Mind Low

Again, the mind and the body are not two things, separate and apart from each other. Where the mind moves, the body follows. It shouldn't surprise you, then, that what happens to your swing, and the ball, are not only determined by your body, but are directly affected by the proper placement of your mind. You can think of it in terms of where the mind goes, the ball goes. When the mind is kept low, the ball maintains a lower ball flight down the fairway. Conversely, when the mind is high, the ball will invariably be lofted into the air where wind and gravity will affect it, and distance is most certainly sacrificed.

> **try this . . .** At the driving range, hit fifteen or twenty balls the way you normally do. Notice the line your ball takes. Is it high? If it is, then it is clear that your mind is high. Now, take a small towel, fold it several times and place it in your belt just below your navel. Then tighten your belt until you feel the pressure of towel against you (see Figure 5A).

FIGURE 5A:
Keeping the Mind Low

Now, proceed and hit another fifteen or twenty balls. What just happened? You will notice that—suddenly—your ball flight is lower, more of a line-drive. This means more distance to your shots. Why? Because instead of the ball spending that time and energy traveling *upward,* it is traveling *outward.* The towel and the tightened belt create a slight pressure just below the navel, which, in turn, draws your mind down to that area. This is what is meant by "keeping the mind low." Whenever you find yourself lofting the ball, you can bet that the mind is the culprit; you can be sure that your mind is high.

try this . . . You can replace the folded towel by using the Bamboo Breath Principle when addressing the ball. To do this, simply exhale through your mouth in short "puffs." As you do, you will notice a gradual tightening of the abdominal muscles. When your exhalation is complete, you may breathe normally, but try to maintain the sense of tightness in your abdominal region. This will keep your mind low and produce those beautiful long drives and fairway shots you want.

Power Principle Addressing the Ball: Oneness with the Earth

If you have a problem "pushing" your drives and approach shots, problems with swing rotation, power, or balance, then you can be sure that by installing "Oneness with the Earth" into your stance the cure is at hand.

Does this sound familiar: You prepare to tee-off and address the ball. You place the club head on the ground behind the ball and then it begins. What begins? The golfer's "Dance of the Seven Veils." You lift your left foot, then your right foot, then your left foot, and again your right, back and forth, forth and back. Then, once that's finally done, you lift your left toes, then your right toes, then your left toes and then your right, over and over again. That's the golfer's ritual "Dance of the Seven Veils!" The problem here is that you are more interested in making yourself comfortable than balanced. Think about it. You could argue that balance is part of the comfortability you're searching for when you "dance," but, in truth, are you really balanced, or just simply balanced "enough" to take your shot?

After you have completed your ritual dance and have found your stance, relax everything: your head, neck, shoulders, torso, arms, and legs. Just let them go limp. When you do this, you will feel the weight of your body "sinking" into the earth; your feet will be flat on the ground and you will have the feeling that they are "welded" there (see Figure 5B). Once you have this "welded" feeling, slowly sway your body (without raising your feet) from your left foot to your right foot, back and forth a few times to further "sink" into the earth. You should now have the feeling of being well planted, your stance is now strong; you are now truly balanced and are poised to draw your strength from the earth.

Power Principle on the Back Swing: Yield and Return

Normally, the typical golfer begins his back swing at the address position, then turns or swings the club to the top of the swing, and eventually reaches what I call the "zero" point. That is, his or her back swing reaches a point of "zero" movement just before it begins its journey forward. We call this back swing a "yielding" movement. The problem is that the power stored up in the back swing is allowed to dissipate in the transition from back swing to down swing. Not only to prevent this dissipation of power, but to actually be able to use it, there should be a smooth subtle "turning" or circular

FIGURE 5B:

Oneness with the Earth

motion of the club at the top of the swing. That is, at the top of the swing, your hands should describe a small vertical, circular clockwise movement, thereby effectively eliminating a point of "zero" movement in your swing. This small turning movement takes the back swing, and smoothly connects it to the down swing, lending the down swing a great deal of added power (see Figure 5C).

Power Principle
on the Down and Through Swing:
The 30–70% Acceleration Principle

When a golfer becomes too impact-conscious, it is the nature of the lower mind to slow down the speed of the club head just before contact with the ball. To overcome this deceleration and to create an "explosive" striking of the ball, there must be an "explosive" acceleration of the club. To achieve this, you will employ 30% acceleration in the first 25% of your down swing and then "explosively" add or "inject" the remaining 70% of your acceleration from that point into your follow through.

FIGURE 5C:
Yield and Return

try this . . . To get the sense of this 30–70% Acceleration Principle, go to the practice range, and using your driver, address the ball. Begin your backswing as slowly as you can—an exaggerated slowness—about 30% of your normal speed. Just after it turns into the down swing, suddenly "inject" as much power as you can into it (that is, the remaining 70%, see Figure 5D). This sudden acceleration will literally "punch" the ball with an explosion of power. Feel this "explosion," like the earth-shaking sonic boom of a passing jet. As you become more familiar with the feeling of this "explosive" power, you should gradually, speed up your back swing and down swing, using this principle, and still feel that explosiveness. The positive results will be very clear to you when you witness the yardage that you have just added onto your drives. This exercise can, of course, be practiced with any of your woods.

FIGURE 5D:
The 30–70% Acceleration Principle

Power Principle at the Point of Impact:
Club Face Alignment

At the point of impact, it is very important that the face of the golf club strike the ball squarely at a ninety-degree angle (see Figure 5E). This will transfer maximum power to the ball. Any deviation in the angle will reduce the contact power, and send the golf ball off-line in relation to the intended target.

The "Void-Through-Void" Principle

In the martial arts, we achieve a great deal of power by passing our hand-strikes and kicks "through" our intended targets. The Void-Through-Void Principle prevents our power from stopping and dissipating on the surface of the object we are striking. It should be no different in golf. You do not want any of your power stopping and dissipating on the outer surface of the ball. In order to achieve this "step-up" in power, you must take the time to visualize both the club head and the ball as being nebulous, or cloud-like. When you strike, you will visualize the cloud-like club head passing completely through the cloud-like ball, cloud-through-cloud . . . void-through-void.

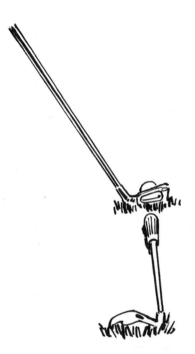

FIGURE 5E:
Club Face Alignment (attaining ninety-degree angle)

The "Nothing to Do" Principle

When I shoot an arrow into a paper cup at a distance of a hundred yards, I am not really doing anything. Why? Because the arrow is already in the cup before I let it go. As a golfer, you must visualize your ball already in the cup even before your club head makes contact with the ball, hence we say, "There is nothing to do!" Why? Because it is already done. You must understand that whenever the physical body is involved in any sort of "striking," whether it is with bare hands or with a weapon (or, in this case, a golf club), the lower mind has a tendency to slow down the strike just before it reaches the target. By using the "Nothing To Do" principle, we trick the lower mind into believing that the immediate target or ball is not only already struck, but is already in the cup. When this principle is incorporated into your game, the lower mind will no longer slow the speed of the club. This principle will not only increase your accuracy, but, when mastered, will also increase your power by keeping your mind relaxed, which in turn will relax your body and allow more power to flow through you.

Breathing

Proper breathing means proper power. In golf, not many players pay attention to their breathing. In the martial arts, on the other hand, breathing is of prime importance. How one breathes will determine whether or not one's power is flowing in the proper direction. Proper breathing is not difficult to use in your game. In fact, proper breathing is really very simple. The rule is: *Inhale on the back swing; exhale on the down swing.*

Exhaling on the down swing will also aid in the Oneness Principles and further insure that "everything is moving down range."

CHAPTER 6

Achieving "The Zone"

MANY OF THE professional athletes who have come to me, at one point or another, invariably have spoken to me of what they call the "zone." They say that when they are in the "zone," their performances are absolutely flawless and without effort; they can do no wrong. They all agree that the problem is that they cannot maintain or summon the "zone" at will, and so are often left to the only viable alternative they have: to put all their effort, all their strength, into their games. When I explain to them that the "zone" they speak of is always present, and can be brought to bear at will in their games, they are speechless. Speechless, that is, until I explain how to access it. They then, magically, turn into loquacious chatterboxes, stimulated by the joy of their newfound revelations, and I often have great difficulty getting them quiet.

The "Zone"—What is It?

An amateur or professional athlete enters the "zone" when his ordinary lower mind is so quiet that his higher mind takes over. As I mentioned earlier, the lower mind is that part of you that contains your fears, hopes, joys, sorrows, dreams and imaginings. It is capricious to a fault, prone to error, and is the greatest deterrent, not only to your being able to access the "zone," but to your peace of mind and general well-being in life, too. The higher mind, on the other hand, is reliable, stable, extraordinarily alert, faultless in design, and miraculously flawless in operation. It is a source of great peace, power, and effortlessness. It is the higher mind that takes command of an athlete's actions when he or she is in the "zone."

How to Access the Zone in Three Steps

Consuming prodigious amounts of alcoholic beverages, inhaling aromatic pine tar, licking a thousand mint-flavored postage stamps, smoking various illegal and suspect substances, trysting with Prince Valium, or shaking a voodoo rattle over your head under a waterfall is not going to do it. The only way to enter the "zone" is to quiet the lower mind.

Look at this scenario and tell me if it sounds the least bit familiar to you: You labor like a demon all week in your office looking forward with great zeal to the weekend when you can hit the links and play a relaxing round of golf. Finally "golf" day rolls around and there you are, steeped in glorious sunshine, fresh air, and the best manicured Mother Nature environment on the planet, and what happens? Just as you are about to tee-off, various uncontrollable thoughts pop into your head, and you begin to worry about your swing, slicing, hooking, topping-off, undercutting, driving short, looking foolish, or you start thinking of your business, your bills, your plans for next week, your neighbor's brand new stereo, and wondering if your cat is pregnant.

Being in the "zone" is being here and now, doing what you are doing at the time you are doing it. There should be no thoughts of anything else—in fact there should be no thoughts at all—just the pure doing of the act.

If you put into practice the following three steps, you will be able to access the "zone" at will and quite effortlessly.

Step 1: Putting Everything Down

The first step to accessing the "zone" is to put all your burdens down; that is, all the things that you carry with you and interfere, not only with your game, but your peace of mind as well.

There is an old story. Zen monks in training at a monastery are not supposed to have any contact, whatsoever, with women. In fact, they are not even allowed to speak to them. One morning, just before sunrise, a young monk and an old monk were on their way back to the monastery from the local village. Just after sunrise they came to a small stream. Standing by the stream was a beautiful geisha dressed in a bright red silken kimono. She was afraid of ruining her kimono in an attempt to ford the stream, and did not know what to do.

Noticing her dilemma, the old monk spoke to her for a few seconds, then lifted her up and carried her across the stream. He gently placed her on the other side. The two monks then continued on their journey to the monastery. They walked all day without a single word between them. Finally, just after sunset, they reached the monastery gate. The young monk could not keep silent any longer and turning to the old monk said, "How could you?"

"How could I what?" replied the old monk.

"You know that we are not allowed to have anything to do with women while we are in training," said the young monk, "How could you pick up that woman this morning and carry her across the stream?"

Smiling, the old monk replied, "How could *you!*"

"How could I what?" answered the puzzled young monk.

"This morning, at sunrise, I picked the geisha up, carried her across the stream and then I put her down. You have been carrying her all morning, all afternoon, and into the evening. When are *you* going to put her down?"

Do you understand? How many geishas do you carry? How often have these geishas of yours interfered with your golf game? Let go of them. How? By keeping yourself in the present, just doing what you are doing; it's that simple. Concentrate on the office when you're in the office. When you are hitting the ball, that should be all that exists in your world . . . put your geishas down and let them go their own way.

Step 2: Focus

In Torishimaru Aiki Jutsu, we refer to focus as "centering." "Centering" as the term implies means to be in the exact middle of things; that is, to be here and now. All that should concern you is your present shot, not the shot that you have just taken, and not the next shot. The game of golf is just one stroke at a time. To begin to "center" yourself you must come to terms with this concept and accept it. To think of the game any other way would not only be deceiving but would keep you out of the place that you want to be: in the "zone."

Listen! In a Zen monastery in Japan, there once was an old monk who frightened all the young monks. They were frightened of him because nothing seemed to bother him; and this bothered them. No matter what would happen, his serenity went uncompromised. It so happened that the old monk's task was to carry a tray of tea each night at midnight to the Master's cottage. In order to accomplish his task, the old monk had to take a path that wound through a small section of woods. One night the young monks conspired to play a nasty trick on the old monk in order to test his serenity. They decided they would hide in the shadows by the path the old monk took, and at the right time, jump out and scare him.

Just before midnight, all the young monks were in place waiting for the old monk to make his appearance on the path carrying the tray of tea. At midnight, the old monk came down the path. At the right time, all the young monks leaped out of the shadows screaming like banshees. The old monk didn't bat an eyelash, and continued serenely on his way. The young monks couldn't believe their eyes at the old man's composure. Sparked by curiosity, they decided to follow the old monk. They quietly followed him down the path some distance. When the old monk came to a small bench along the path, he stopped, and gently placed the tray of tea on it. Then, he reached inside of his sleeve, took out a large handkerchief and, bending, placed it over the tray so that no dust would ruin the tea. Then, suddenly, to everyone's amazement, the old monk, grabbed his chest, screamed as if he were suddenly terrified, and reeled backward several steps. Then, having screamed and reeled, the old monk serenely walked over to the tea, removed the handkerchief, picked up the tea tray and quietly continued on his way. Needless to say, the young monks were stunned, and never tried to disturb the old monk again.

The reason for the old monk's composure is easy to understand. He was focused; he was "in his nowness." That is, when the young monks leaped out of the shadows, the old monk was occupied, carrying the tray of tea. He had no time to be frightened. When the old monk came to the small bench along the path, he put down the tea tray. When he did, he found that he now had the time to be frightened and so, in mock fear, for the benefit of the young monks that he knew were watching, he clutched his chest, screamed and jumped back. If you are truly focused on what you are doing, in the time that you are doing it, there will be no time to be frightened, frustrated, or anxious. When you tee-off, just tee-off; when you putt, just putt, and you will experience Nowness and be *centered*. It sounds simple, but it takes practice and patience. The rewards will be reflected not only in your golf game, but in your life as well.

Important: The following two techniques, the Heart Sephira Technique and the 60-Second Meditation, are both very simple to execute, but don't be fooled by their simplicity. They are extremely effective in proper centering. Use them, practice them, and you may be pleasantly surprised at the results.

The Heart Sephira Technique

Many years ago, as the result of deep and protracted meditations, a great many spiritual insights came to me that proved enormously valuable in furthering my understanding of the nature of the world and my own personal relationship to the matrix of existence. The Heart Sephira Technique is just one result of those many insights.

I named it the Heart Sephira Technique because we are injecting *M'retz Na'she,* or power, into a spiritual gate or *sephira* located over the heart area. I cannot emphasize enough the importance of this technique. It is not only the fastest meditation I know, but contains an element of power transfer uniquely suited to the golfer deeply involved in the competitive rigors of the game. Take the time to learn this technique and apply it to each and every stroke just prior to addressing the ball. If you dismiss this technique out of hand, you will be doing both yourself and your game a great disservice. Trust this technique, it will not fail you! You will experience the positive results of employing this technique immediately. The Heart Sephira Technique *makes* champions!

1. Before each and every stroke-just before you address the ball-place the open palm of your right hand on the Heart Sephira as shown in Figure 6A, page 105.

2. Take a deep inhalation, breathing in that fresh, golf-course air, and hold your breath for three to five seconds. Do not rush to hit the ball.

3. Exhale slowly sending the breath through your "hollow" arm, then through your palm and into the Heart Sephira.

4. Now address the ball.

Benefits:

- Supplies the Heart Sephira with M'retz Na'she or power.

- Clears and calms the lower mind, ridding it of extraneous and unwanted thoughts.

- Eases tension and relaxes body muscles, translating into more power.

- Separates your current stroke from the previous stroke, and the current stroke from the next.

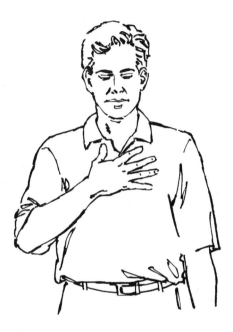

FIGURE 6A:
The Heart Sephira Technique

The 60-Second Meditation

This is a quick meditation technique that can be practiced while you are riding in the golf cart or walking to the ball for your next shot. It brings serenity and clarity to the mind-something so important not only to playing excellent golf, but to the general enjoyment of the game. Do not underestimate its value. Trust it and use it.

1. Stop your thoughts and clear your mind by exhaling (through your nose) as much air as you can. When you have squeezed out all the air, hold your breath for a few seconds. You will notice that all your thoughts disappear.

2. Begin to breathe in, through your nose, very slowly. Follow your breath as it enters your body. Allow that breath to fill your body as if your entire body were "hollow."

3. Exhale and follow your breath as it leaves your body.

4. Continue this exercise until you reach your ball.

Step 3: Just Doing

At this point, you are ready to address the ball and take your shot. "Just doing" is just that: just doing; that is, leaving everything up to your higher mind. Having just centered yourself using the Heart Sephira Technique, your lower mind should be calm and your higher mind placed in a dominant position. Everything that you need to know, everything that needs to be done is already recorded on your higher mind tape, so just let it happen. You must trust your higher mind to get it done. We say in the martial arts, "When there is nothing to do, everything gets done." The more you think there is to do, the more there "is" to do. There should not be any thinking, just the doing, just the stroke. You must trust yourself, you must trust your higher mind to make that perfect shot. If you do, you may be pleasantly surprised at the results.

try this . . . To experience the sense of "just doing" on the golf course; address the ball and start to sing aloud. That's right, sing! Sing anything you like, "Mary Had a Little Lamb," "Battle Hymn of the Republic," "Dixie," it doesn't matter what, just sing as you take your shot and watch what happens. Watch how suddenly both your power and accuracy increases. Why? Because when you are singing you are occupying your lower mind, leaving the shot up to your higher mind, and there is no choice. I know that you may feel a little self-conscious about singing, but I have had a number of very well known and accomplished tour players singing at one point or another during their training, and they too felt self-conscious at first, but changed their attitudes when they saw the results.

try this . . . Find an area of the driving range where you can tee-up ten balls side-by-side spaced approximately six to eight inches apart. Then, with the first ball on your left, while singing, and as quickly as you can, with your driver, fire each ball down range. You must be able to send all ten balls down range without interrupting your song. In this exercise, you cannot spend too much time addressing the ball. I tell my students to imagine that the balls are ten hand grenades with the pins pulled out of them. They may explode at any time and that they only have a few seconds to dispose of them using only the club in their hands. In this exercise, again, the singing artificially occupies the lower mind "forcing" the higher mind to take charge. It is a way of testing the information recorded on the higher mind tape for correct technique.

Naturally, a player who has come to understand the concept of "just doing" doesn't and shouldn't need to rely on singing to help get him into the "zone," but for those who need it, for those who await understanding, it is there for them to use.

CHAPTER 7

Playing the Fairway

WHAT YOU ARE about to learn—once you've experienced it—will change your golf game forever. It will not only broaden you, but will alter the very nature of your perspective of the course. However, I must preface the instruction with the following plea: You must keep an open mind! If you do, you will be doing both yourself and your game an immeasurably wonderful service.

Sensing the Course—the Pull of the Fairway

Everything in existence is surrounded by a force-field that we in Torishimaru Aiki Jutsu call the "shield." The shield affects everything around it by offering a natural resistance to movement in a very subtle, yet palpable way. These shields affect one's mind in relationship to those objects. For example, in the martial art I teach, we often fight blindfolded in the Master's ranks. The shields surrounding our bodies allow us to locate our attackers' presence. My shield senses the subtle pressures offered by their shields. When you practice the exercise below, you will experience the subtle pressures offered by the trees lining both sides of the fairway and the draw of the vacuum existing between them. When experienced and applied, techniques involving the shield will always keep your ball on the fairway and forever out of the rough.

To begin with, you need to experience your own shield, so take both of your hands and place them in front of you a few inches apart, palm facing palm. Then very slowly begin to "pump" them back and forth, toward and away from each other. You will feel a slight pressure existing between them, as if you were trying to place the two like-poles of magnets together. That sensation is your own shield and the subtle pressure that a shield produces (see Figure 7A).

> **try this . . .** You are at the tee, facing the fairway. On either side of the fairway are trees. Turn slightly to the trees on your right and lean very slightly into them with your chest. Then turn, while continuing to lean toward the center of the fairway. Once you have "cleared" the trees you should experience a sudden release of pressure on

FIGURE 7A:

Experiencing Your Own Shield

your body causing you to fall forward (see Figure 7B). This sudden release of pressure is caused by what I call a "feminine vacuum." This feminine vacuum not only "pulls" your body, but more importantly, will pull your mind down the center of the fairway. In golf we call this the "Pull or Draw of the Fairway." Also try this with the trees to your left. Remember, where the mind moves, your body will move; where your mind moves, your ball will move. The "Pull of the Fairway" will draw your mind right down the center and this is where your mind should be. *Note:* This principle should be applied throughout your game, from tee-off to green. After practicing this principle it will soon become part of you, and will occur very naturally and quickly. In fact, after practice, just a glance will be sufficient to bring about the Pull of the Fairway.

In sensing the "Pull of the Fairway," you will automatically sense the resistance offered by various obstacles on the course. When this happens, you will immediately sense the vacuum or "pull" existing around those obstacles. Your mind will feel the

FIGURE 7B:
Sensing the Pull of the Fairway

draw of those vacuums and automatically calculate a viable path for the ball to travel. Naturally it takes some practice, but if you lend yourself to it, you should experience the "Pull of the Fairway" the very first time you try it.

Playing the Wind

Let's face it, you are in the great outdoors, and being outdoors your game is subject to the whims of nature. One of those whims, often, is the unpredictability of the wind. For example, the wind may be blowing rather hard where you are, and yet, may not be blowing down range. When this happens you may find that your attempt to compensate for the wind turns out to be exaggerated and your ball lands somewhere deep in the rough. Or perhaps there is a subtle, almost negligible breeze blowing, and as you look down range at the pin, the flag is hardly budging. Feeling certain that all is well, you don't compensate for the wind. You fire your shot only to discover there is a stiff wind blowing forty feet off the ground, which takes your ball and places it thirty feet from where you intended it to go. These are not uncommon scenarios out on the course, even among touring pros. This is where the all-important attributes of the higher mind comes in. Remember, the higher mind knows all things: past, present, and future. It is the intuitive part of your being. This is where you should turn over the calculations to the higher mind. By using the Heart Sephira Technique, you will subtly quiet your lower mind, allowing your higher mind to take over. You must trust your higher mind to make the proper adjustments in order to place your ball where you want it. Trust your higher mind.

The Grip

The particular grip you use, overlap, interlock, 10-finger, etc., is largely a personal choice (see Figures 7C–7E, pages 121–123). Still, you must keep in mind that the grip is the point where your breath and power are transferred from the earth, through your hollow body and arms, to the club. Regardless of the grip you use, you should never grip the club with all of your strength. On the contrary, you should use only enough strength to give you control over the club. When you grip the club too tightly, you are tensing not only the muscles of your hands, but also the muscles of your forearms, upper arms, shoulders, and chest. Tensing these muscles will not only greatly reduce your power but, unless your grip is consistent, you will be prone to many slices and hooks. Remember, when your muscles tense they create an inward pull toward your own body. This will translate in the club moving slightly toward your body when you swing, resulting in a slice. If you look to compensate for the slice, and your grip is suddenly less tense, it will result in a hook. So your grip must be consistent and relaxed. When it is, not only will your swing become more consistent, but more strength will flow through you and your ball will travel much farther.

try this . . . Tee-up and hit several drives gripping the club as tightly as you can and notice what happens. Then, relax your grip, tensing just enough to control the club, and drive the ball. Can you feel the difference? Can you see the difference? The relaxed grip translated into more power, resulting in more distance.

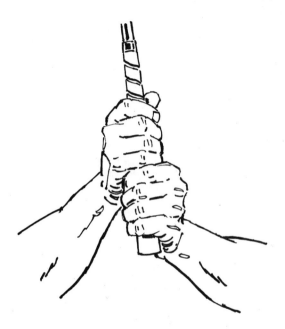

FIGURE 7C:

10-Finger Grip

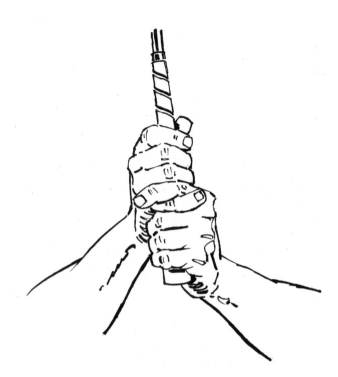

FIGURE 7D:
Interlocking Grip

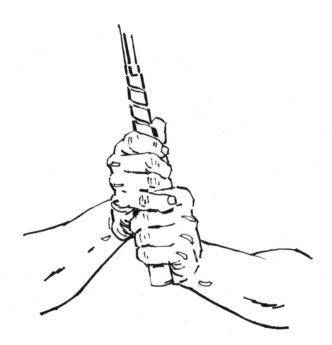

FIGURE 7E:

Overlapping Grip

Ball Position

Never tee the ball too high. The higher you tee the ball, the more of a chance you have of undercutting and lofting the ball (see Figure 7F). This, of course, translates into less distance and power. Also, you should tee the ball in a consistent manner. This will reduce another element that may lead to inconsistencies to the ball each time you tee off.

Driving

Below are listed elements that, when learned and practiced, will give your drives that championship look and performance. This is a time-tested formula that will change your game for the better. Each of the steps listed can be introduced into your drives as you learn them. When all eight elements are finally part of your drives, you will be driving the ball with the best of them!

1. Use the Heart Sephira Technique (see pages 103–105) to center yourself just before your stroke.

2. Use the Pull of the Fairway Principle and go for distance, the accuracy will be there.

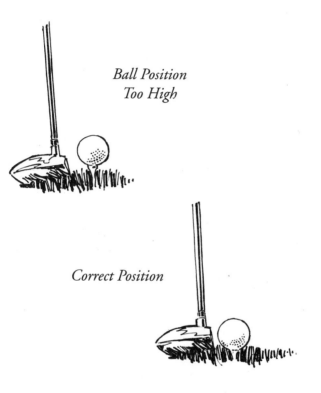

*Ball Position
Too High*

Correct Position

FIGURE 7F

3. Proper Breathing. Inhale on the back-swing, exhale on the forward swing.

4. Use the 30–70% Acceleration Principle.

5. Use the Oneness with the Earth Principle. Avoid rocking and lifting the balls of your feet.

6. Allow your mind to lead your movement. Where the mind goes, your body follows; where the body goes, the ball will go.

7. Keep your mind low—in the Hara (just below the navel).

8. Don't tee the ball up too high, and try to be consistent with the tee height each time you tee off.

Pitching

The following five elements will lead to "super" pitching. Learn them, employ them, and trust them. You will not be sorry!

1. Use the Heart Sephira Technique to center yourself just before your stroke.

2. Any club you choose to pitch with is to be considered an extension of yourself. You, the club, the ball, and the hole are One. (see Oneness with the Earth Principle, pages 82–84.)

3. Send your mind to the spot that you want the ball to land on within the "funnel" you created by using the Funneling Principle described in the putting section of this book ("On the Green," page 133).

4. After the ball lands, it will roll. Employ the Putting Principles (Chapter 8: "On the Green").

5. Be fearless, and allow the higher mind to take control of the pitch.

Chipping

Chipping onto the green should be considered as nothing more than an exciting variation of putting. Don't be like those golfers who are joyous over that fact that they were able to place their ball, after chipping, within a few feet of the hole. You must consider the chip shot an extended putt. Never settle: be fearless!

1. Use the Heart Sephira Technique to center and relax yourself just before your stroke.

2. Any club you choose to chip with should be considered an extension of yourself. You, the club, the ball, and the hole are One.

3. Send your mind to the spot that you want to land on within the "funnel" you create by using the Funneling Principle described in the putting section of this book.

4. After the ball lands, it will roll. Employ the Putting Principles.

Bunker Play

The existence of bunkers is one of the factors that makes the game of golf so challenging. When faced with the challenge of a bunker shot, follow the following formula and all will be well:

1. Use the Heart Sephira Technique to center and relax yourself just before your stroke.

2. Your mind's eye or higher mind should see the club pass under the ball allowing the ball to "float" out of the bunker and onto the green.

3. Allow the sand to throw the ball out of the bunker.

4. Send your mind to the spot that you want to land on within the "funnel" you create by using the Funneling Principle described in the putting section of this book.

5. Don't fear the sand!

Trouble Shots

Thick rough, ball in divot, bare or hard pan lies, uphill lies, downhill lies, side-hill lies, as well as obstacles such as water hazards and trees, are all examples of trouble shots. They are some of the elements that make the game of golf what it is. Bear the following in mind when you are facing them:

1. Don't allow your mind to paint pictures about the trouble spot you find yourself in.

2. Remember, the fact that trouble spots exist on the golf course is, to a great extent, what makes the game so challenging. Accept the challenge and enjoy the game.

3. Employ the Heart Sephira Technique to center and relax yourself just before your stroke.

4. Don't be afraid to take chances. Once you have quieted your lower mind by employing the Heart Sephira Technique, you must trust your higher mind to do the right things. Remember, trusting the higher mind is important, all your training is recorded there.

CHAPTER 8

On the Green

The Funneling Principle

THIS PRINCIPLE IS designed to both bring your mind to, and then keep your mind focused on, the cup. Practicing this principle on the practice green requires eight poker chips or coins. Place them in two angular lines on either side of the cup forming a "funnel" shape (see Figure 8A, page 135). All you have to do is stroke the ball within the funnel. You will find that this will give you great accuracy not only on your shorter putts but especially on those long difficult putts. Naturally, on the course, the use of poker chips is replaced by visualizing the "funnel." Everything lying outside of the funnel should be completely ignored, since it has nothing to do with your present putt.

The White-Line Principle

Drop the ball anywhere on the practice green and imagine a white line approximately three inches wide extending from the ball to the front lip of the cup. When used in conjunction with the Funneling Principle, it forms an arrow pointing directly to the cup. On your shorter putts, ten feet or less, all you have to do is stroke the ball along this white line and into the cup. You must stroke the ball hard enough to keep it on the white-line.

Using the White-Line Principle requires only the adjustment of the ball speed. The pitch of the green does not have to be considered. A firm pace imparted to the ball by the putter-head will roll the ball along that white line. A good aggressive putt will hold its line to the hole, especially on breaking putts. When negotiating right-to-left or left-to-right breaking putts, simply adjust the white line and funnel to visualize the break, but always bear in mind the sudden death mentality (where every putt is a "win or lose" putt), and stroke it firmly.

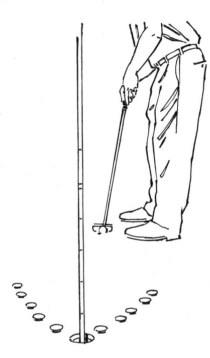

FIGURE 8A:

The Funneling Principle

The Pendulum Principle

Choose a putter that allows you to stand over the ball rather than out and away from the ball. Allow the putter to swing like a pendulum from your shoulders, and not from your wrists (Figure 8B). This allows the larger, more dependable muscles to control the flow and pace of the pendulum action. A freely swinging pendulum always takes a straight and undeviated path.

When used in conjunction with the White-Line Principle, and a great deal of practice, your number of putts per round average will certainly plummet down. It is important, however, that you do not grip the putter too tightly; simply allow the putter to swing freely like a pendulum. Let the club do the work. It's that easy.

FIGURE 8B:
The Pendulum Principle

The Seven Elements to Great Putting

Use them and you will be enormously trimming your stroke count per round. Trust them!

1. Use the Heart Sephira Technique (see page 103–105) to center yourself just before your stroke.

2. Keep the sudden death mindset at all times.

3. Use the Funneling Principle.

4. Use the White-Line Principle.

5. Never lag the ball. Always "go for the gold!"

6. Pendulum putter action by using the Pendulum Principle.

7. When putting off the green, have no fear. *Just do it!*

CHAPTER 9

Optional Advanced Meditation

FOR THOSE WHO desire to take advantage of the enormous benefits that longer and more formal meditation will add to their golf game, I have included some advanced meditation exercises in this chapter. These meditations are optional, but I highly recommend them. They will not only change your golf game for the better, but if practiced, will change your life too. They can be done in the privacy of your home, or anywhere you feel comfortable, a private room at the country club, a secluded area by a lake, or at the beach at sunrise or sunset.

Meditation Postures

I teach five fundamental *asanas* or meditation positions: *seiza, full lotus, half lotus, Burmese style,* and *lenient* (see Figures 9A–9E, pages 143, 145–148). Seiza is the traditional Japanese kneeling posture. In seiza, one assumes a kneeling position resting the buttocks on the heels. If one is using a pillow, or *zafu*, then it is

141

placed between the ankles, edge up (see Figure 9A, page 143), and the buttocks rest on that. Position your knees two fist-widths apart (see Figure 9A inset, page 143) and keep your back erect, but not rigid. The head is aligned vertically with the chin tucked slightly inward.

Your hands form the *universal mudra* (a very special formation of the hands), with your right hand placed palm-up on your lap with the pinkie sides touching your lower abdomen. Your left hand is then placed palm-up on top of the right hand with both thumbs touching lightly at the tips (see Figure 9B inset, page 145). When this mudra is done correctly the thumbs will complete an oval, as if you held an egg there. Keep your eyelids lowered—but not closed—and your gaze placed on the floor at a distance of approximately five feet. Students of Torishimaru Aiki Jutsu must become very familiar with the seiza posture. It is a traditional posture in my system.

In cross-legged postures, it is always best to use a zafu (or a firm pillow). The zafu supports the spine and, especially for beginners, eliminates unnecessary strain in the lower back area. Also, besides simply being more comfortable, the zafu greatly aids proper posture.

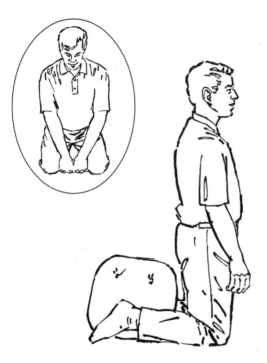

FIGURE 9A:

Sitting for seiza (inset: knees two fist-widths apart)

The full lotus, or *Padmasan* position, is historically, the most difficult of all the sitting postures. Cross your legs with your right foot placed on your left thigh, and left foot on your right thigh. For the beginner, this is normally a very difficult sitting posture because it requires great flexibility in the knee and ankle joints.

In the half lotus, place your left foot on your right thigh with the right leg simply folded underneath. I have always found the half lotus posture preferable for those students with an average amount of flexibility. For those with less flexibility there is the Burmese style, in which the legs are folded with both calves resting flat on the ground, one in front of the other. For those students who are truly inflexible and find it much too difficult to assume the other sitting postures, there is what I call the "lenient" posture, which is simply sitting comfortably with the legs crossed at the ankles in what is familiarly called "Indian" fashion.

In all five postures, the universal mudra is used, both knees must touch the floor, and all the rules for proper head and spinal alignment apply throughout.

FIGURE 9B:

Full lotus position (inset: universal mudra)

FIGURE 9C:
Half lotus position

FIGURE 9D:
Burmese-style position

FIGURE 9E:
Lenient position

Note: There are times and individual circumstances, such as a lack of privacy, that make it not only permissible but simply more convenient to do the meditation while sitting in a chair. When seated in a chair, you must keep your back straight but not rigid and both feet flat on the floor, with your hands forming the universal mudra resting on your lap.

Candle Concentration Exercise

Candle Concentration is an ancient and time-tested exercise. It is not a meditation *per se,* but is one of a number of proven methods often used to bring about a very special state of mind that we call "one-pointedness." In "one-pointedness," all your mental faculties are focused or concentrated on one object. When one practices this exercise long enough, one is able to take this "one-pointedness" and apply it to great benefit, not only in various meditations, but to the game of golf as well. It is an especially good exercise for the beginner.

In a darkened room, place a lit candle approximately three to four feet in front of you. You may do this exercise in any of the meditative postures or, if you prefer, while sitting on a chair with the candle placed on a table in front of you. Stare at the flame for two minutes. While staring at the flame you may notice the different parts of the flame, as well as the flame's various colors. You may blink when necessary. After a short while, you will notice that the flame takes on a "solid" appearance. Continue to concentrate on the flame for an additional two minutes, for a total of four minutes in all. At the end of the four minutes, close your eyes and gently cover them with the palms of your hands. You will now notice the image of the flame in your mind's eye surrounded by a rich field of blackness.

While your eyes are closed and covered, notice the various colors of the image; the yellows, greens, reds, purples, etc. Try to keep the image of the flame focused and centered in your vision. Should the image begin to rise, and it will, you must concentrate and "will" it back down. Should the image blur or in some way go out of focus, you must concentrate and "will" it back into focus. As you continue, you will notice that the colors of the image will change. This is normal. Take note of the various colors as you continue to concentrate on refocusing and recentering the image. Eventually, the image will fade to the point that you think it is gone. When this occurs you must concentrate and try to "will" it back. Continue to do this until you reach the point where the image is gone and cannot be retrieved.

This concentration technique will bring about a marked "retraining" of your lower mind. When practiced properly, it will promote the "one-pointedness" so very necessary to both good meditation and great golf.

Proper Meditation

There are several points to stress in meditating properly. First of all, your body must be physically balanced, not leaning to the left or leaning to the right, and you should not struggle to keep from losing your balance to the rear. This is very important: there should be no slouching to the front. For a beginner this will happen without you realizing it. You must sit with a sense of dignity, a feeling of great majesty, as if you were a great monarch giving audience to your loyal subjects. Also you must have the sense of supporting the infinite sky with the top of your head and keep your chin slightly tucked in.

It is a simple matter to find the balanced center of your posture. Once you assume the meditative posture of choice, simply sway your body gently from side to side in pendulum fashion slowly coming to a stop in the center. Follow with a slow, rocking forward and backward motion, again slowing until physically centered. It is that simple.

Be careful to not fidget. Fidgeting not only throws the body out of alignment, but also has a tendency to "pull" the mind away from the matter at hand. Fidgeting will greatly interfere with a sensation called "body falling away" or *Prateyahara,* and will impede your progress.

Finally, pay the strictest attention to what is required in your particular meditation. Attention to what you are doing is paramount, and cannot be overemphasized. You must be "here" and "now." If your mind wanders, then you are not doing what you are supposed to be doing-you are doing something else. Should this occur, simply bring your attention back to the matter at hand. You should not experiment or make arbitrary changes while meditating; no wandering down the fruitless path of invention. If you follow these instructions, all will be well and your progress will be assured.

Shikan-taza or *"Just Sitting"*

Shikan-taza is the ultimate meditation of the samurai and Zen masters. It will go a long way in improving not only your ability to concentrate on the golf course, but bring you into the pristine state of "nowness," a state that every golfer, especially competitive golfers, must be in, in order to access the totality of his or her talents and skills. Without "nowness" your games will be inconsistent and your scores will suffer.

To practice this meditation at home, you should choose a quiet area of your house, one free of disturbance and interruption. There you should use one of the meditative postures described. Once that has been accomplished and your body is physically centered or balanced, lower your eyelids (do not close them) placing your gaze on the floor approximately five to six feet in front of you. You may blink when necessary. Then begin to concentrate on your posture. That's all, just your physical posture. That is, you attention should be focused on the physical act of sitting, making sure that your head and spine are correctly aligned. When thoughts come to you just let them float by. Do not become attached to them or pay any attention to them, just continue concentrating on your posture. Meditate, initially, in this manner for a period of ten minutes, twice a day. The period of meditation may be increased at the rate of five minutes every two weeks until you are sitting in meditation for thirty minutes a day. It may not seem like you are doing much when you practice shikan-taza, but in reality you are doing a great deal. You are learning to be in your "moment" or "nowness." You are training yourself to be there and then without thoughts of the future or past, a state "devoutly to be wished" by touring pros and all competitive golfers.

A Word About Thoughts During Shikan-taza

When you practice shikan-taza, thoughts are bound to come to you. Thoughts, in and of themselves, are not a problem. The real problem is the nature of those thoughts. For example, if random thoughts come to you, just simply allow them to dissolve, to float by like little white clouds in a clear blue sky.

The problems begin when random thoughts link together to become narratives or stories. For example, there are practicing your shikan-taza when you hear a car door slam outside. This noise produces in you the thoughts: "Is that my car? It sounds like my car. My wife was supposed to have the oil changed. I thought she went to the supermarket. I wonder what we are having for dinner? I hope it's lasagna. I'm too fat, I have to go on a diet. My brother-in-law eats like a horse and is as thin as a rail, etc."

This is a narrative pattern, a pattern that began with a single thought, generated by a random sound: the slamming of a car door, that swept you to thoughts of your car, your wife, food, dieting, and your brother-in-law. It is these kind of thoughts that should be avoided. When they begin, you must recognize them for what they are and return yourself to the matter at hand, which is concentrating on your posture. After a while, you will begin to take charge of your thoughts, and they will dissipate on their own, allowing you total and complete control of whatever you are doing at the moment. It will allow you to hit each shot on the golf course with total concentration, unencumbered by thoughts created out of distraction. It will allow you to be there and then. That is a golfer's dream.

Shikan-taza can be performed just about anywhere. In a doctor's office, while the dentist is working on your teeth, or getting your haircut, or waiting for a train or waiting for your wife to decide what she is going to wear that night. It can be done while sitting quietly on a bench or a chair, and not just in one of the formal sitting postures.

The benefits are waiting for you to reap them in!

QUICK REFERENCE

HERE IS A list of quick reference items you can refer to when you're facing certain difficulties in your golf practice.

Problem	Solution(s)	Page(s)
Imbalance	Oneness with the Earth	82–84
Nervous Tension (Anxiety)	Heart Sephira Technique	103–104
	60-Second Meditation	106
	Dead Man's Pose	41–43
Physical Tension	Heart Sephira Technique	103–104
	60-Second Meditation	106

Problem	Solution(s)	Page(s)
Lofting the Ball	Centering the Hara (see Keep the Mind Low)	79–81
	Oneness with the Target	66
Shots in the Rough	Sensing the Course	113–118
	Heart Sephira Technique	103–104
Lack of Focus/Concentration	Heart Sephira Technique	103–104
Lack of Power	Heart Sephira Technique	103–104
	Oneness with the Earth	82–84
	Oneness with the Target	66
	Centering the Hara (see Keep the Mind Low)	79–81
	Turning the Club	84
	30-70% Acceleration	86–88
Topping the Ball	Oneness with the Earth	82–84
	Oneness with the Target	66
	Centering the Hara (see Keep the Mind Low)	79–81

Problem	Solution(s)	Page(s)
Frustration or Anger	Stopping the Breath (see 60-Second Meditation)	106
	Stop Painting Pictures	54–56
	Heart Sephira Technique	103–104
	60-Second Meditation	106
Shanking the Ball	Heart Sephira Technique	103–104
	Oneness with the Earth	82–84
	Centering the Hara (see Keep the Mind Low)	79–81
Hitting the Ball Flat	Heart Sephira Technique	103–104
	Oneness with the Hole	66
	Oneness with the Earth	82–84
Can't Gauge the Wind	Heart Sephira Technique	103–104
	Trust Your Higher Mind	49

Problem	Solution(s)	Page(s)
Pulling Your Putts Offline	Heart Sephira Technique	103–104
	White-Line Principle	134
	Oneness with Putter, Ball, and Hole	62–68
	Funneling Principle	133
	Pendulum Principle	136
Pushing Your Putts	Heart Sephira Technique	103–104
	White-Line Principle	134
	Oneness with Putter, Ball, and Hole	62–68
	Funneling Principle	133
	Pendulum Principle	136
Rolling Ball Past Hole	Heart Sephira Technique	103–104
	Oneness with the Hole	66
	White-Line Principle	134
	Trust Your Higher Mind	49
Putts Short of Hole	Heart Sephira Technique	103–104
	Oneness with the Hole	66
	White-Line Principle	134
	Trust Your Higher Mind	49

INDEX